C000241565

Free From
Recipes

Compiled by
Carol Wilson
Images by
Trevor Mitchell

Index

Cover Pictures: Front Cover *'Early Birds'*
Back Cover *'The Village Bus Stop'*
Title Page *' Harvest Lunch'*

Printed & published by Dorrigo, Manchester, England © Copyright

Gluten Free Cheese and Herb Bread

This flavoursome bread is yeast free and is delicious served warm or at room temperature. It also makes great sandwiches.

320g gluten free plain flour, 1 tbsp gluten free baking powder
1½ tsp bicarbonate of soda, 1 tsp salt, 1 tsp dried sage, ¾ tsp dried thyme
350ml gluten free beer, 2 tbsp honey
55g strong Cheddar cheese, finely grated
55g Parmesan cheese, finely grated, 2 tbsp butter, melted

Set the oven to 190°C (170° fan) gas mark 5. Grease a 23cm x 11cm loaf tin and line the base with non-stick baking paper. Stir together the flour, baking powder, bicarbonate of soda, salt and herbs in a mixing bowl and make a well in the centre. Pour in the beer and honey and mix until only just incorporated. Add the cheese and mix until well blended. Spoon into the tin and drizzle the melted butter over the top. Bake for 35-45 minutes until golden brown and a skewer inserted into the centre comes out clean. Cover with foil for the last 15-20 minutes of cooking, to prevent overbrowning. Cool in the tin on a wire rack for 10 minutes, before turning out onto a wire rack to cool completely.

Gluten and Dairy Free
Chicken Korma

This Indian dish of tender chicken in a creamy, mildly spiced aromatic sauce made with coconut milk is full of flavour. Serve with boiled rice.

2 tsp olive oil, 1 onion, peeled and quartered, 2 cloves garlic
2 tsp ground coriander, 1 tsp ground turmeric
½ tsp ground ginger, ½ tsp ground cumin, 1 pinch salt, 1 pinch sugar, 2 curry leaves
2 lime leaves, 1 tsp coriander seeds, 55g ground almonds
3 skinless boneless chicken breasts, cut into bite-size pieces, 400ml coconut milk
2 cardamom pods, lightly crushed, flaked toasted almonds (optional)

Put the oil, onion, garlic, ground coriander, turmeric, ginger, salt and sugar in a blender or food processor and blend to a smooth paste.   Put into a pan with the coriander seeds and heat over a medium heat and stir for 1 minute.   Stir in the curry leaves, lime leaves and coriander seeds and cook, stirring for 2-3 minutes. Add the ground almonds and chicken and keep stirring for a further minute, until the chicken is coated with the mixture.   Stir in the coconut milk and cardamom pods, then cover the pan and simmer over a low heat for 20-25 minutes, until the chicken is cooked through, with no trace of pink.   Stir and remove the cardamom pods.   Place in a serving bowl and sprinkle with flaked almonds if liked.

Five

Gluten Free Herb Fish Cakes

You can use any white fish – e.g. cod, haddock, whiting, for these tasty fishcakes. Serve with lemon wedges.

300g white fish fillets, 400ml milk
2 sprigs parsley, leaves chopped, stalks reserved, 8 black peppercorns, 2 bay leaves
450g potatoes, peeled and chopped into even-sized pieces, Salt, 4 spring onions, finely chopped,
1 unwaxed lemon, finely grated zest, 1 handful rocket, roughly chopped
2 sprigs dill, chopped, freshly ground black pepper, cornflour for dusting,
3 - 4 tbsp vegetable oil, for frying

Put the fish in a frying pan. Cover with the milk; add the parsley stalks, peppercorns and bay leaves. Cover, bring to the boil, then reduce the heat and simmer for 4 minutes. Remove from the heat, cover the pan and leave to stand for 10 minutes. Put the potatoes into a pan and just cover with water. Add the salt, bring to the boil, and then cook for 10-15 minutes, until tender. Drain and roughly crush. Set aside to cool. Lift the fish out of the milk with a slotted spoon and put onto a plate to cool. Flake the fish and discard any bones or skin.   Add the spring onions, lemon zest, rocket and dill to the potatoes with salt and pepper to taste. Mix together, continuing to break up the potatoes, but without creating a smooth mash.   Add the fish to the potato and herb mixture. Roll the mixture into balls. Lightly dust the balls with cornflour, pat and flatten into fishcakes. Heat the oil in a large frying pan. Fry the fish cakes for 4- 5 minutes on each side, until crisp and golden. Drain on absorbent kitchen paper.

Gluten Free Ham and Mushroom Pizza

Home made pizza is much nicer than shop bought and this appetising pizza has a base made with polenta (cornmeal) and is easy to make.

For the base: 790ml water, 1 tsp salt, 200g polenta, 2 tbsp olive oil, freshly ground black pepper
For the topping: 1 tbsp olive oil, 1 onion, finely chopped, 2 cloves garlic, finely chopped
400g tinned chopped tomatoes, 1 tsp sugar, salt, freshly ground black pepper
1 tsp chopped thyme, 55g mushrooms, thinly sliced
100g cooked ham, thinly sliced, 100g mozzarella cheese, sliced
50g parmesan cheese, finely grated, 2 tbsp olive oil

For the base: line a large flat baking tray with non-stick baking paper.   Heat the water to boiling in a large pan. Add the salt. Slowly add the polenta and stir. Reduce the heat and continue stirring for about 5 minutes, until thickened.   Pour in the oil and stir to incorporate. Add the black pepper to taste and stir well. Spread the polenta evenly into a large round on the baking tray. Cover and chill for about 1 hour until set. Set the oven to 200°C (180° fan), gas mark 6.

For the topping: heat the oil in a frying pan and gently cook the onion for a few minutes until softened. Add the garlic and cook for 1 minute. Add the chopped tomatoes, sugar, salt and pepper to taste. Bring to a simmer and cook for 4-5 minutes until thickened. Remove from the heat. Spread the tomato mixture on the pizza base and sprinkle with thyme. Arrange the mushrooms, ham and both cheeses on top. Drizzle with half the oil and season with salt and pepper.   Bake for 20-25 minutes until the edges are golden and the cheese has melted. Drizzle with the remaining oil.

Gluten Free Fennel Gratin with Nut Crust

Delicious on its own, the slight aniseed flavour of fennel also goes really well as an accompaniment to roast meats or fish dishes.

2 large fennel bulbs, sliced in half lengthways, salt
1 tbsp olive oil, 2 cloves garlic, finely chopped, 570ml tinned chopped tomatoes
1 pinch sugar, lemon juice, freshly ground black pepper
2 tsp fennel seeds, 125g walnuts, chopped
6 tbsp grated parmesan cheese, butter

Set the oven to 180°C (160° fan), gas mark 4. Lightly grease 2 medium baking or gratin dishes. Put the fennel halves into a pan of boiling salted water and cook for 7-10 minutes until tender when pierced with the point of a skewer. Drain well. Heat the oil in a frying pan and cook the garlic for 2-3 minutes until softened. Stir in the tomatoes and sugar and cook, stirring until slightly thickened. Season to taste with lemon juice, salt and pepper and stir in the fennel seeds. Pour into the baking dishes and place the fennel halves on top. Sprinkle with the walnuts and cheese, then dot with butter. Bake for 15-20 minutes until the cheese is bubbling.

Trevor Mitchell

Gluten Free and Vegan Green Vegetable Risotto

This delicious risotto makes a lovely light meal in spring or summer

2 tbsp olive oil, 2 shallots, finely chopped
1 clove garlic, crushed, 200g arborio rice
850ml hot vegetable stock
12 runner beans, sliced diagonally and steamed
1 bunch asparagus, trimmed of any tough stems
300g frozen peas, 2 tbsp chopped mint, 50g vegan cheese, grated, salt and pepper

Heat the oil in a wide pan and cook the shallots and garlic very gently until soft but not brown. Add the rice and stir until the rice becomes translucent then add a ladle of hot stock and stir until it is absorbed by the rice. Reduce the heat and continue adding the stock one ladle at a time, stirring constantly, until the rice has become creamy and just cooked through. You may need to add a little more stock or water. Steam or boil the runner beans and asparagus for 5-7 minutes, until tender. Drain and set aside. Add the peas, mint and cheese to the risotto, season with salt and pepper and continue cooking for about 2 minutes until the peas are cooked through. Serve the risotto topped with the runner beans and asparagus.

Dairy Free Macaroni Cheese

The ultimate comfort food makes a great supper dish served with a simple green salad. There are a wonderful variety of completely dairy and lactose free cheeses available from most supermarkets.

275g dairy free alternative to cheddar cheese, grated, 55g fresh breadcrumbs
1 pinch salt, 300g macaroni, 700ml soya or rice milk
50g dairy free margarine, 50g plain flour, 1 tsp dijon mustard

Set the oven to 190°C (170° fan), gas mark 5. Grease a baking dish, about 30 x 20 x 5.5 cm. Mix 55g of the cheese with the breadcrumbs. Set aside. Bring a large pan of water to the boil. Add the salt and macaroni, stir and return to the boil. Simmer for 8 minutes, or cook according to the packet instructions, stirring occasionally to prevent sticking. Warm the milk. Melt the margarine in a large pan and stir in the flour. Cook for 1 minute, stirring, then remove from the heat. Pour in 1/3 of the warm milk and beat well until smooth. Add another 1/3 of the milk and continue beating well until smooth. Pour in the final 1/3 of milk and beat until smooth. Heat the sauce, stirring, until thickened and smooth. Reduce the heat and simmer for 3-4 minutes until shiny. Remove from the heat and stir in the remaining cheese and mustard. If the sauce is too thick, add a little more soya milk. Drain the macaroni in a colander and rinse under hot running water. Drain well, and then gently stir into the sauce to coat completely. Tip the macaroni cheese into the baking dish and scatter over the cheese breadcrumbs. Bake for about 15-20 minutes until beginning to bubble around the edges. Heat the grill. Grill for 5 minutes to brown the crumbs. Serve immediately.

Trevor Mitchell

Dairy Free Pasta Bake

This mouthwatering creamy pasta bake is made with oat cream, an alternative to dairy cream, that's free from lactose, milk protein and soya

20g dried porcini mushrooms, boiling water, 2 tbsp olive oil
4 boneless skinless chicken thighs, cubed, salt, freshly ground black pepper
2 cloves garlic, finely chopped, 350g mushrooms, chopped
200ml dry white wine, 320g spaghetti, 500ml oat cream
150g dairy free hard cheese, grated

Set the oven to 200°C (180° fan), gas mark 6. Grease a large baking dish. Put the porcini mushrooms in a bowl and pour over just enough boiling water to cover them. Set aside to soak for a few minutes. Heat the oil in a large pan. Season the chicken pieces with salt and pepper and brown them gently in the oil. Strain the porcini, reserving the soaking water and add the porcini to the pan with the garlic and fresh mushrooms. Add the wine and the strained porcini soaking water, then reduce the heat and simmer gently until the chicken is cooked through and the wine has reduced a little. Cook the spaghetti in a pan of boiling salted water according to the packet instructions and drain well. Add the oat cream to the chicken mixture. Bring just to the boil, and then remove from the heat. Season well with salt and freshly ground black pepper. Add the drained spaghetti to the chicken sauce and mix well. Add 3/4 of the cheese and stir well. Put into the baking dish, sprinkle with the remaining cheese and bake for 15-20 minutes until golden brown and bubbling.

Dairy Free Toad in the Hole

One of the classic English dishes, this easy delicious recipe is ideal for lunch or dinner.

2 tbsp vegetable oil
450g dairy free pork sausages
225g plain flour
1 pinch salt
3 eggs
230ml oat milk
150ml water
2 - 3 tsp chopped thyme

Set the oven to 220°C (200° fan), gas mark 7. Heat 1 tablespoon oil in a frying pan and fry the sausages for 5 minutes until browned on all sides. Heat the remaining oil in a large baking dish or roasting tin in the oven until very hot. Put the flour and salt into a mixing bowl and make a well in the centre. Whisk together the eggs, oat milk and water beating well until smooth. Pour into the well and add the thyme, beating until smooth. Place the sausages in the dish or tin and pour over the batter. Bake for about 30 minutes until risen and puffy. Serve immediately.

Dairy Free Tomato Quiche

This tasty quiche is delicious eaten warm or cold and is perfect for a picnic or light lunch with salad. You can use any dairy free milk, e.g. oat, soya, etc. but make sure it's unsweetened.

**For the pastry: 225g plain flour, plus extra for dusting, 150g dairy free margarine
1 egg yolk, 1 pinch salt. For the filling: 225g baby spinach, 4 eggs, 300ml non dairy milk, salt and pepper
175g dairy free hard cheese, grated, Freshly ground black pepper, 125g cherry tomatoes, halved
1 tbsp vegetable oil**

For the pastry: sift the flour into a mixing bowl. Rub in the margarine until the mixture resembles bread-crumbs. Beat in the egg yolk and salt until the mixture just comes together as a dough. If the mixture is too stiff, add a little water. Roll the dough into a ball, then wrap in cling film and chill for 30 minutes. Set the oven to 190°C (170° fan) gas mark 5. Grease a 23cm springform flan tin. Roll out the pastry on a floured surface and line the tin. Prick the pastry all over with a fork, line the pastry case with non-stick baking paper and fill it with rice or dried beans. Bake for 10 minutes, then remove the paper and beans. For the filling: put the spinach in a large pan, with just the water clinging to the leaves after washing. Cover tightly and cook over a low heat for 3-5 minutes, until wilted. Drain in a sieve, then squeeze out the water. Chop the spinach coarsely. Whisk together the eggs and milk and season to taste with salt and pepper. Mix in the spinach and half the cheese. Put the filling into the pastry case, levelling the surface. Toss the halved cherry tomatoes in just enough oil to coat them, then arrange over the top of the filling, cut side uppermost. Grind over a little black pepper and sprinkle with the remaining grated cheese. Bake for 30-35 minutes until the filling has set and is lightly golden. Remove the sides of the tin and leave to stand for 10 minutes before serving.

Dairy Free Fish Pie

Use any type of fish such as cod, haddock, salmon, etc. for this creamy fish pie with a fluffy potato topping.

For the topping: 1kg potatoes, cut into chunks, 120ml soya milk, 100g dairy free margarine
salt and pepper. For the filling: 400g fish fillets, cut into bite sized pieces, 1 bay leaf, 4 peppercorns
1 onion, quartered, 450ml soya milk, salt, freshly ground black pepper
2 spring onions, roughly chopped, 75g dairy free margarine
3 tbsp plain flour, 1 tbsp finely chopped parsley

For the topping: put the potatoes into a large pan, cover with cold salted water and bring to the boil. Simmer for 20 minutes or until the potatoes are tender then drain, return the potatoes to the pan and add the milk and margarine. Heat for 3 minutes, then turn off the heat and mash until smooth and lump free. Season to taste with salt and pepper. Set the oven to 200ºC (180ºC fan) gas mark 6. For the filling: put the fish into a large pan and add the bay leaf, peppercorns, onion and soya milk. Season with salt and black pepper and simmer very gently for 10 minutes. Remove any skin from the fish and divide the flesh between a large baking dish or 4 ovenproof dishes, along with the spring onions. Strain the milk from the pan through a sieve and set aside. Melt the margarine in a pan, add the flour, stir until smooth and cook for 1 minute. Add about 250ml of the strained milk, bring to the boil and simmer for 5 minutes, stirring all the time, until the sauce has thickened. Season with salt and pepper, stir in the parsley and pour over the fish. Top with the mashed potato, spreading it out evenly and roughing the top. Cook for 30-35 minutes for the large baking dish and 20 minutes for the smaller dishes, until golden brown and piping hot.

Vegan Chilli sin Carne (Chilli without meat)

This tasty vegetable chilli is packed with flavour. The cocoa powder and Marmite add a deep rich flavour. You can increase or reduce the amount of chilli powder, depending on how spicy you prefer your chilli. Serve with boiled rice

**175g green lentils, boiling water, 2 tbsp vegetable oil, 1 large onion, chopped
2 cloves garlic, crushed, 1 - 2 tsp chilli powder, 2 tsp cocoa powder
1 tsp ground cumin, 1 tsp Marmite, 2 red peppers, seeds removed and chopped
800g tinned chopped tomatoes, 1 tbsp tomato puree
300ml vegetable stock, 100g peas, 1 courgette, chopped
salt, freshly ground black pepper, 400g tinned red kidney beans, drained**

Put the lentils in a large bowl and pour boiling water over them to cover. Leave to soak for 30 minutes. Drain well. Heat the oil in a large pan and cook the onion, garlic, chilli, cocoa and cumin over a low heat for 7-10 minutes or until the onions are soft, but not browned. Add the Marmite, peppers and drained lentils and cook for 5 minutes, stirring all the time. Add the tomatoes, puree, stock and peas. Bring to the boil and simmer gently for about 30 minutes until the lentils are tender. Add the courgette and simmer for a further 5 minutes. Season to taste with salt and pepper. Add the drained kidney beans and simmer for 5 minutes.

Vegan Spicy Cous Cous Cakes

These are delicious as a snack, appetizer or for a light lunch with salad.

**250g couscous, 250ml boiling vegetable stock, 2 tbsp vegetable oil
1 large parsnip, grated, 1 carrot, grated, 1 small onion, finely chopped
salt, to taste, freshly ground pepper, to taste, 1 tsp grated lemon zest
1 tsp cumin seeds, 1 tsp turmeric, 1 pinch ground coriander
1 - 2 tbsp tahini, 2 - 3 tbsp plain flour**

Put the couscous in a large bowl and pour over the stock. Leave to swell for 20 minutes, then break up with a fork. Set the oven to 180°C (160° fan) gas mark 4. Line a large baking tray with non-stick baking paper. Heat the oil in a frying pan and cook the parsnip, carrot and onion for a few minutes until soft, then remove from the heat. Stir into the couscous with the salt, pepper, lemon zest, cumin, turmeric, coriander and tahini. Stir in the flour until a pliable dough is formed. Shape the couscous dough into small patties and place on the baking tray. Bake for 15-20 minutes until golden.

Vegan Vegetable Curry

This thick wholesome curry combines healthy vegetables and warming spices- far better than a takeaway! Serve with naan bread.

**2 tbsp olive oil, 1 red or green chilli, finely chopped, 2 tbsp grated root ginger, 1 tsp mustard seeds
1 tsp cumin seeds, 5 curry leaves, 1 tsp ground turmeric, 1 tsp curry powder, 1/2 tsp salt
3 sweet potatoes, peeled and cut into cubes, 200g ripe tomatoes, quartered
1 small cauliflower, divided into florets, 1 courgette, thickly sliced, 1 tsp lemon juice
1/2 tsp sugar, 2 tbsp water, 2 tbsp chopped coriander**

Heat the oil in a pan over a medium heat until hot, then add the chilli, ginger, mustard and cumin seeds, curry leaves, turmeric, curry powder and salt. Stir well and cook for 2 minutes, or until the seeds start to pop and the spices smell fragrant. Add the sweet potatoes and stir well, then add the tomatoes, cauliflower, courgette, lemon juice, sugar and water and bring to the boil. Reduce the heat, cover the pan and simmer gently for 20-25 minutes, until the vegetables are cooked and the mixture has thickened. If the vegetables start to stick, add a little water. Sprinkle with the coriander and serve immediately.

The Village Station

Vegan Onion Flatbread

Spicy flatbreads make a wonderful accompaniment to soup or a vegetable curry

450g strong white (bread) flour, plus extra for dusting
1 tsp salt, 20 g fresh yeast
280ml warm water
1 onion, finely chopped, 1 tsp ground cumin
2 tsp ground coriander
2 tbsp olive oil

Sift the flour and salt into a mixing bowl and make a well in the centre. Cream the yeast with a little of the water, then mix in the rest of the water. Add the yeast mixture to the centre of the flour and mix well to a firm dough. Turn out onto a lightly floured surface and knead for about 10 minutes until smooth and elastic. Put the dough into a lightly oiled bowl and cover with oiled cling film. Leave in a warm place for about 1 hour, until doubled in size. Lightly grease 2 baking trays. Turn out the dough onto a lightly floured surface and knead lightly. Divide into 8 pieces and roll each piece in a 13-15cm round. Prick all over and place, well apart on the baking trays. Cover with oiled cling film and leave to rise for 15-20 minutes. Set the oven to 200°C (180° fan) gas mark 6. Mix together the onion and spices. Brush the risen dough rounds with olive oil and sprinkle the onion mixture on top. Bake for 15-20 minutes until lightly golden. Serve warm.

Vegan Vegetable Paella

This substantial Spanish-inspired paella is full of flavour. Do use a special Spanish rice that absorbs large amounts of the liquid without becoming creamy or sticky, as in risotto. Smoked paprika imparts a depth of flavour, which is unique to Spanish cuisine.

**2 1/2 tbsp olive oil, 2 cloves garlic, crushed, 1 large onion, finely chopped
1 stick celery, finely chopped, 2 firm tomatoes, peeled and chopped
100ml boiling water, ½ tsp saffron threads
300g Calasparra or paella rice, rinsed and drained
1 tsp smoked paprika, 700 - 800 ml vegetable stock, 1 large carrot, diced
225g green beans, trimmed chopped to ½-inch lengths
1 red pepper, seeds removed, diced, 150g peas, salt and pepper, 180 g black olives, pitted**

Heat 2 tablespoons of the olive oil in a paella pan, or deep wide frying pan. Add the garlic and cook for 1 minute, then add the onions and celery. Cook gently until softened, then add the tomatoes and cook for 5 minutes. Add the saffron to the boiling water and stir well, then add to the pan and simmer for 3 minutes. Add the rinsed rice to the pan with the paprika, stock and saffron water and saffron threads. Bring to a simmer and cook for 10 minutes. Add the carrots, green beans and red pepper. Cook for 20 minutes, then stir in the peas and continue cooking, stirring occasionally, until the rice is tender and the stock absorbed. Add a little more stock or water if the mixture is too dry. Season to taste with salt and pepper and stir in the olives.

Gluten Free Orange and Blueberry Cake

Moist, golden and sweet, this delicious cake is perfect to serve at an afternoon tea.

300g butter, 300g caster sugar
1 large unwaxed orange, grated zest and juice, 4 eggs
200g ground almonds
180g polenta (cornmeal), 2 tsp gluten free baking powder
100 ml plain yoghurt, 200 g blueberries

Set the oven to 180°C (160° fan) gas mark 4. Grease a 23cm round cake tin and line the base with non-stick baking paper. Beat together the butter, sugar and orange zest in a mixing bowl until light and creamy. Beat in the eggs, one at a time, alternating each addition with a quarter of the ground almonds. Add the orange juice, polenta, baking powder and yoghurt and stir well. Stir in half the blueberries. Spoon into the tin and sprinkle the remaining blueberries over the top. Bake for about 50-60 minutes until a skewer comes out clean when inserted into the centre of the cake. Cover loosely with foil if the cake becomes too dark during cooking. Cool in the tin for 10-15 minutes, then place on a wire rack to cool completely.

Trevor Mitchell

Gluten Free Chocolate Pear Cake

Pears add a lovely flavour to this moist chocolate loaf cake

**60ml milk, 1 tsp cider vinegar
1 ripe pear, peeled, cored and chopped, 1 tbsp lemon juice, 112g butter
112g caster sugar, 2 very ripe bananas, mashed well
60g plain chocolate (70% cocoa solids) melted and cooled
60g sweet rice flour, 60g sorghum flour
3 tbsp cocoa powder, 1 ¼ tsp gluten free baking powder, 1 - 2 tbsp grated chocolate**

Set the oven to 180°C (160° fan), gas mark 4. Grease a 450g loaf tin. Mix together the milk and vinegar and set aside. Toss the pears in the lemon juice. Beat together the butter and sugar in a mixing bowl until light and creamy. Add the mashed banana gradually, beating well after each addition. Add the melted chocolate and beat until smooth. Add the milk mixture and beat until incorporated. Add the flours, cocoa and baking powder and beat until blended. Pour into the tin and smooth the top. Sprinkle with the pears. Bake for 30-40 minutes until cooked through. Cover with foil if the cake is browning too much as it cooks. Sprinkle the top of the warm cake with a little grated chocolate. Cool in the tin for 15 minutes, then place on a wire rack to cool completely.

Gluten Free Carrot Cupcakes

Light, fluffy and moist, these carrot cupcakes are topped with a cream cheese topping flavoured with orange juice.

For the cupcakes:
225g light muscovado sugar, 3 large eggs
200ml sunflower oil, 225g gluten-free self raising flour
1 tsp ground cinnamon, 1 pinch salt, 350g carrots, grated, 175g walnuts, chopped

For the topping:
225 g cream cheese, 2 tbsp light muscovado sugar
1 tbsp orange juice, ground cinnamon

For the cupcakes: set the oven to 180°C (160° fan), gas mark 4. Place paper cases in a 10 hole muffin tin. Beat together the sugar, eggs and oil in a mixing bowl until light and frothy. Stir in the flour, cinnamon and salt and stir until combined. Stir in the carrots and walnuts. Spoon into the paper cases and bake for 20-25 minutes until firm and risen. Place on a wire rack to cool.

For the topping: beat all the ingredients together until smooth. Chill for 30 minutes. Spread the topping over the top of the cakes and dust with a little cinnamon.

Trevor Mitchell

Gluten Free Peanut Butter and Puffed Rice Squares

These no-bake indulgent sweet treats are quick and simple to make. You can use plain puffed rice cereal and smooth peanut butter instead of crunchy if you prefer.

90g cocoa puffed rice cereal
397g tin sweetened condensed milk
125 g crunchy peanut butter
112ml golden syrup
110g light muscovado sugar
60g roasted unsalted peanuts, chopped

Grease and line the base of a 23cm square tin with non-stick baking paper. Put the cereal into a large bowl. Heat the condensed milk, peanut butter, syrup and sugar in a pan until just melted. Stir well and stir in the peanuts. Pour over the cereal and mix well until the mixture binds together. Press into the tin with dampened hands and smooth the top. Cover with cling film and chill for 2 hours until firm. Cut into squares to serve.

Twenty-Nine

Gluten Free Raisin Bread

A sweet fruity bread, with a hint of spice. It's delicious serve sliced, spread generously with butter. It's great toasted too.

350g gluten-free strong white (bread) flour, 150g raisins
2 level tsp fast-action dried yeast, 1 tbsp ground cinnamon
1 tsp caster sugar, 1 tsp salt
l tsp xanthan gum, 250ml milk
1 large egg, 4 tbsp sunflower oil
1 tsp cider vinegar

Grease a 450g loaf tin. Put the flour into a mixing bowl and stir in the raisins, yeast, cinnamon, sugar, salt and xanthan gum and mix well. Mix together the milk, egg, oil and vinegar.   Pour the milk mixture into the flour and mix well, to give a soft dropping consistency.   Spoon the mixture into the tin and level the surface. Cover the tin loosely with oiled cling film and leave in a warm place to rise, until it has risen above the top of the tin.   Set the oven to 220°C (200° fan), gas mark 7. Bake for 30-40 minutes, or until it sounds hollow when tapped underneath, covering with foil if it starts to brown too quickly. Remove from the oven and place the loaf on a wire rack to cool.

Dairy Free Chocolate Ice Cream

Everyone will love this delicious dairy and egg-free chocolate ice cream made with coconut milk

800 ml tinned coconut milk, 75 g caster sugar
90g honey, 1 ½ tsp vanilla extract
1 generous pinch salt, 50g cocoa powder, 3 tsp cornflour
100g plain chocolate (70% cocoa solids) roughly chopped

Pour half the coconut milk into a heavy-based pan and stir in the sugar, honey, vanilla extract and salt and heat gently until the sugar has dissolved completely. Whisk in the cocoa powder, whisking until fully incorporated. Put the cornflour in a separate bowl and very slowly whisk in the remaining coconut milk, a little at a time, making sure there are no lumps. Stir this into the pan over a medium heat until the mixture begins to bubble gently. Cook for a few minutes, stirring constantly, until the mixture thickens. Remove from the heat and add the chocolate, stirring constantly, until completely melted. Place a sheet of cling film or non-stick baking paper directly onto the surface of the mixture to prevent a skin forming and leave to cool, then chill until completely cold. Churn the chilled mixture in an ice cream maker according to the manufacturer's instructions. Alternatively, pour into a freezerproof container and freeze for 40 minutes, beating with a fork to break down the ice crystals. Repeat this process twice more during freezing, to break up the ice crystals. Tip the mixture into a food processor and process until smooth. Return to the container, cover and freeze for 2-3 hours until firm. Remove from the freezer 15 minutes before serving to soften slightly. *Thirty-One*

Dairy Free Cherry Trifle

A sumptuous boozy trifle that can be made in 1 large bowl or individual serving dishes.

For the custard: 300ml rice milk, 2 tbsp custard powder
200ml coconut milk, 2 tbsp sugar

For the base: 10 - 12 dairy free sponge cake or fingers, 1 - 2 tbsp cherry jam
4 tbsp cherry brandy, 425g tinned cherries in syrup, drained, 135g pack cherry jelly

For the topping: 300ml coconut cream, well chilled, toasted flaked almonds

For the custard: mix a little of the rice milk with the custard powder to a paste. Heat the remaining rice milk, coconut milk and sugar in a pan, stirring until the sugar has dissolved. Whisk in the custard powder mixture and bring to the boil. Cook, whisking for 2 minutes until thickened. Pour into a bowl and cover the surface directly with cling film. Set aside to cool.

For the base: cut the cake into thin slices and sandwich with the jam, or sandwich the sponge fingers in pairs with the jam. Break into pieces and put into the base of a serving bowl or 4-6 serving glasses. Sprinkle with cherry brandy. Spoon the cherries evenly on top. Make up the jelly according to the pack instructions. Leave to cool slightly then pour on top of the sponge fingers, pressing them down into the jelly. Chill until set. Spoon the custard on top of the jelly. Whip the chilled coconut cream until thick and spread over the custard. Sprinkle with flaked almonds.

Trevor Mitchell

Dairy Free Strawberry Mousse

A fruity dessert that's light and fluffy and very easy to make

400g strawberries, sliced, plus extra to decorate
400g firm silken tofu, drained
3 tbsp agave syrup

Puree the strawberries in a blender or food processor until smooth. Press through a sieve to remove the seeds, then return the puree to the food processor. Gradually add the tofu, a little at a time and blend until incorporated. Add the agave syrup and process for 1-2 minutes until light and creamy. Spoon into serving bowls and chill for at least 1 hour until firm. Decorate with strawberries.

Dairy Free Chocolate Fudge

This smooth, rich chocolatey fudge would make a perfect gift for someone who is unable to tolerate dairy.

6 tbsp dairy free margarine
370g icing sugar
65g cocoa powder
1 tsp vanilla extract
60ml soya or non-dairy milk

Grease a 20cm square tin and line the base with non-stick baking paper. Place the margarine, sugar, cocoa, vanilla and milk in a heatproof mixing bowl. Place the bowl over a pan of simmering water and stir until the margarine is fully melted and the mixture is completely smooth. Pour the mixture quickly into the tin. Chill for 2-3 hours until set. Cut into squares and store, chilled, in an airtight container for up to two weeks.

Sugar Free Coconut and Cardamom Desserts

Delicious little desserts sweetened with Xylitol- a natural sweetener with 40% fewer calories than sugar and which is also safe for diabetics.

400ml tinned coconut milk
100ml milk
10 cardamom pods, seeds only, ground
60g semolina
60g xylitol

Mix together the coconut milk and milk in a pan. Sprinkle in the ground cardamom and bring to the boil. Whisk in the semolina and beat well until smooth. Reduce the heat, add the xylitol and simmer for a few minutes to thicken. Pour into serving glasses and chill for at least 2 hours before serving.

Sugar Free Lemon Loaf Cake

A fresh tasting lemon cake, free from refined sugar. It's sweetened with coconut palm sugar made from the sap of the coconut palm. The sugar is extracted from the palm by heating it until the moisture evaporates. After processing, the sugar has a caramel colour and tastes like brown sugar. Coconut palm sugar is considered a healthier option, as it contains less fructose than other sweeteners.

250g plain flour, 2 tsp baking powder, ¼ tsp salt, 170g coconut palm sugar
2 tbsp agave syrup, 70ml sunflower oil, 250ml milk
2 tsp cider vinegar, 1 unwaxed lemon, 2 tbsp juice and finely grated zest

For the drizzle:
2 - 3 tbsp agave syrup, 2 tbsp lemon juice

Set the oven to 180°C (160° fan), gas mark 4. Grease a 13cm x 23cm loaf tin and line the base with non-stick baking paper. Sift the flour, baking powder and salt into a mixing bowl and stir to combine. Whisk together the sugar, syrup, oil, milk, vinegar and lemon juice, then stir in the lemon zest. Pour into the dry ingredients and stir until well mixed. Put into the tin and bake for about 40 minutes, until a skewer inserted into the centre comes out clean. Cool in the tin for a few minutes then place on a wire rack. For the lemon drizzle: stir together the syrup and lemon juice until blended. Poke holes in the cake with a skewer. Gently spoon the syrup over the top of the cake and leave to cool completely.

Sugar Free Apple Cheesecake

A lovely lightly spiced cheesecake made with fresh apples, which makes a perfect dessert or a teatime treat.

For the filling: 500g cottage cheese, 500ml Greek yoghurt, 2 cooking apples, peeled, cored, sliced
50g coconut palm sugar, 1 tsp ground cinnamon, 4 tbsp clear honey, 1 large egg
1 tbsp cornflour, 1 tsp vanilla extract, few drops green food colouring, optional
For the pastry: 200g plain flour, plus extra for dusting, 125g butter, 1 pinch salt, water

For the filling: put the cottage cheese into a food processor and blend until smooth. Stir in the yoghurt and spoon the mixture into a muslin-lined sieve set over a bowl. Cover with cling film and chill for 12 hours to drain off the excess liquid. Heat a large frying pan over a medium heat. Toss the apple slices with the sugar and cinnamon and add to the pan. Cook for 4-5 minutes, shaking the pan occasionally to prevent the apples from burning, until the apples are tender. Place the apples on a tray to cool. Tip the yoghurt mixture into a clean bowl, discarding the liquid. Beat in the honey, egg, cornflour and vanilla. Beat in the colouring if using.

For the pastry: mix the flour and salt in a mixing bowl and rub in the butter until the mixture resembles breadcrumbs. Gradually add just enough water to form a dough. If the dough is crumbly, add more water. If it is wet and sticky, add a little more flour. Form the dough into a ball, wrap in cling film and chill for 1 hour. Set the oven to 170°C (150° fan), gas mark 3. Grease a 22cm-23cm deep springform flan tin. Roll out the dough on a lightly floured surface and line the base and sides of the tin. Arrange the apples on the pastry base. Pour in the filling. Bake for about 45 minutes until the edges are set but the centre is still slightly wobbly. Cool completely in the oven, then remove and place on a serving plate.

Sugar Free Walnut Cake

A lovely moist cake sweetened with honey. You can use any type of honey – using different honeys, e.g. dark and rich such as heather honey or light, such as acacia will vary the flavour.

175g butter
165g runny honey
1 unwaxed lemon, finely grated zest
75g ground walnuts, 3 eggs
100g wholemeal flour
3 tsp baking powder
55g walnut halves

Set the oven to 170°C (150° fan), gas mark 3. Grease a 9cm x 19cm loaf tin and line it with non-stick baking paper. Put the butter, honey and lemon zest in a bowl and beat with an electric whisk until light and fluffy. Add the ground walnuts and then the eggs, one at a time, beating well after each addition. Sift the flour and baking powder into the bowl and fold gently into the mixture. Spoon into the tin and smooth the top. Scatter over the walnut halves. Bake for about 45-50 minutes, until a skewer inserted into the cake comes out clean. Remove from the oven and cool in the tin for 10 minutes, then place on a wire rack to cool completely.

Trevor Mitchell

Pumpkin Spice Muffins
Gluten Free, Sugar Free, Dairy Free

Pumpkin makes these tasty muffins light and moist. Coconut palm sugar is made from the sap of the coconut palm. The sugar is extracted from the palm by heating it until the moisture evaporates. After processing, the sugar has a caramel colour and tastes like brown sugar. Coconut palm sugar isconsidered a healthier option, as it contains less fructose than other sweeteners.

**75ml sunflower oil, 225g coconut palm sugar 55ml rice or soya milk, 1 tsp vanilla extract,
150g gluten free plain flour ½ tsp gluten free baking powder, ½ tsp bicarbonate of soda
¼ tsp salt, ¼ tsp ground cinnamon, ¼ tsp grated nutmeg
225ml tinned pumpkin puree**

Set the oven to 180°C (160° fan), gas mark 4. Place paper cases in a 12 hole muffin tin. Whisk together the oil, sugar, milk, and vanilla in a mixing bowl. Sift in the flour, baking powder, bicarbonate of soda, spices and salt. Gently whisk until well combined. Fold in the pumpkin, but do not over mix or the mixture will become 'gummy'. Spoon into the paper cases and bake for 20-25 minutes, until risen and golden. Cool in the tins for 5 minutes, then place on a wire rack to cool completely.

Vegan Banana and Walnut Bread

Deliciously moist with plenty of banana flavour. Make sure you use very ripe, almost black bananas

3 large very ripe bananas, mashed
75ml sunflower oil
100g light muscovado sugar
225g self-raising flour
2 heaped tsp baking powder
3 tsp mixed spice
50g walnuts, chopped

Set the oven to 180°C (160° fan), gas mark 4. Grease a 1kg loaf tin. Mix together the bananas, oil and sugar until blended. Add the flour, baking powder and spice and mix well. Stir in the walnuts. Spoon into the loaf tin and bake for 50- 60 minutes until golden and risen. Cover with foil if the cake is browning too quickly. Cool in the tin for 10 minutes, then turn out onto a wire rack to cool completely.

Vegan Brownies

Rich, fudgy brownies with a deep chocolate flavour make a luxurious indulgent treat

255g plain flour, 150ml water
350g extra firm silken tofu
175 g plain vegan chocolate (70% cocoa solids) chopped
400g sugar, ½ tsp salt, 2 tsp vanilla extract
110 ml sunflower oil, 75g cocoa powder
75g nuts, walnuts, macadamia nuts or almonds, chopped

Set the oven to 180°C (160° fan), gas mark 4. Grease an 18 x 28 cm baking tin and line the base with non-stick baking paper. Puree the tofu, 75g flour and water in a blender or food processor until smooth. Pour into a pan and whisk constantly over a low heat until thickened. Do not boil. Remove from the heat and stir in the chocolate, salt, vanilla and sugar until the chocolate has melted. Set aside to cool for 30 minutes. Stir in the oil until smooth and then stir in the cocoa, remaining flour and nuts until blended. Put into the tin and spread evenly. Bake for 35-40 minutes until cooked but the centre is still a little soft to the touch. Cool in the tin. Cut into squares to serve.

Vegan Strawberry and Banana Muffins

These light fluffy muffins are packed with fresh strawberry and banana flavours. The ingredients are stirred until only just combined to make the muffins light in texture. Don't overstir!

112ml soya yoghurt, 2 very ripe bananas, mashed
1 tsp vanilla extract
112g vegan margarine, melted
250g plain flour, 175g sugar
1 ½ tsp baking powder, ¼ tsp bicarbonate of soda
¼ tsp salt, 150g strawberries, sliced

Set the oven to 180°C (160° fan), gas mark 4. Place paper cases in a 12 hole muffin tin. Stir together the yoghurt, mashed bananas and vanilla. Stir in the margarine. Sift the dry ingredients into a mixing bowl and gently fold in the strawberries, making sure they are coated with flour. Add the wet ingredients to the dry ingredients and stir until just combined. Spoon the mixture into the paper cases. Bake for 20-25 minutes, until golden and risen. Place on a wire rack to cool completely.

Vegan Panna Cotta

This delicious light, sweet and creamy dessert can be served on its own or accompanied by fresh berries. Do use full-fat coconut milk

225ml soya or almond milk
400ml tinned coconut milk
1 tbsp agar flakes
115g sugar
1/8 tsp salt
1/2 tsp vanilla extract

Lightly grease 6-8 ramekins. Combine all the ingredients except the vanilla in a pan. Stir and leave to stand for 10 minutes before heating. Slowly bring to the boil. When it starts to boil, reduce the heat and simmer for 5-8 minutes until the agar dissolves. Remove from the heat and stir in the vanilla. Pour the mixture into the ramekins, then chill uncovered in the refrigerator for 3-4 hours until set. Run a knife around the sides and slide onto serving plates.

Metric Conversions

The weights, measures and oven temperatures used in the preceeding recipes can be easily converted to their metric equivalants. The conversions listed below are only approximate, having been rounded up or down as may be appropriate.

Weights

Avoirdupois	Metric
1oz	Just under 30 grams
4oz (¼ lb)	approx. 115 grams
8oz (½ lb)	approx. 230 grams
1lb	454 grams

Liquid Measures

Imperial	Metric
1 tablespoon (liquid only)	20 millilitres
1 fl. oz	approx. 30 millilitres
1 gill (¼ pt)	approx. 145 millilitres
½ pt	approx. 258 millilitres
1 pt	approx. 570 millilitres
1 qt	approx. 1.140 litres

Oven Temperatures

°Fahrenheit		Gas Mark	°Celsius
Slow	300	2	150
	325	3	170
Moderate	350	4	180
	375	5	190
	400	6	200
Hot	425	7	220
	450	8	230
	475	9	240

Flour as specified in these recipes refers to plain flour unless otherwise described.